T0273206

Herbaceous

PAUL EVANS

Illustrated by
Kurt Jackson

A LITTLE TOLLER **MONOGRAPH**

Paperback edition published by Little Toller Books in 2018

Little Toller Books, Lower Dairy, Toller Fratrum, Dorset

First published by Little Toller Books in 2014

Typeset in Berling and Perpetua by Little Toller Books

Printed by TJ International, Padstow, Cornwall

All papers used by Little Toller Books are natural, recyclable products made from wood grown in sustainable, well-managed forests

A catalogue record for this book is available from the British Library

ISBN 978-1-1908213-59-4

For Maria Nunzia

Contents

Illustrations

HERBACEOUS *adj* resembling or having the nature of herbs (any non-woody seed-bearing plant which dies down to the ground after flowering but whose roots etc. survive); a state or quality of being characterised by such plants.

DART

MARSH
MARIGO

Yellow

Lesser celandine

By a holly tree on a distant hill, a bitten-off piece
of the lunar eclipse is buried under the mound, a
blind staring from the earth. The dark tree marks
time at a nameless crossing as black flies touch the
first yellow celandines. All obligations, however lost
or forgotten, must be honoured.

Trout lily

Air in the March woods tastes of bourbon nipped
from a hip flask, fiery yet cold as the brook over a
frozen stick dam. At two o'clock in the morning,
the Onion Towners come down to do their
shopping in the Grand Union. They holler, running
up and down, catching tins and packets thrown
over from parallel aisles in their trolleys, then drive
back to tarpaper shacks in the hills. At dawn, thin
and grey is the timber, like sunlight through barn
slats and then a sudden flood of yellow all down
the Appalachians. Fish-leaved and bell-jiggled, lilies
grow from the forbidden land.

Cowslip

These flowers come from shit, so the story goes;
that's our story, too. Beautiful, beautiful then.
We gathered them, balled them, tossed them like
wedding knots. We tied them to the tails of our
cattle, to the poles of our May; we carried keys-of-
heaven* to open the primrose path with all that joy,
such sweetness. Now we've reached the end of it?
Well. . .

* 'Happen you call it cowslip, but we always named it the
paigle or keys of heaven,' Mary Webb, *Precious Bane* (1924).

Wallflower

Yellow wallflowers stunned by frost. Blackcaps, jittery around empty bird feeders are perhaps the first generation of their kind without a memory of migration. The ground is dry with a strange violet-grey dustiness and freeze-thickened mud. The weather forecast, full of predictions for conflict between warm Atlantic air clashing against cold Russian air, uses that same angst-ridden tone the news speaks of politics in. Ill-humoured petulance pushes us further into climate anxiety where the weather is adversarial. Out of a puddle-grey sky, the wind brings the first hint of snow, chill and sweeping in all directions. In the woods, a fall of invisible hail crackles like static through bare branches. In the open, the wind roars darkly through pines, soughs in the ash and hisses around limes and oaks. Small birds – bluetits and great-tits squeak in treetops and wrens plump up like bobbles – scarper into the undergrowth. A ratty-winged buzzard trying to get back to a safe haven is intercepted by a raven in a brief ritual skirmish.

A gang of jackdaws fling themselves from a lone tree into the wind and back. Out on the Edge, between the woods and the fields, the wind ice comes needling, pricking exposed skin. It's a couple of hours before this turns to snow but it's only a loose swirl of ten-pence-sized flakes and it softens into white quiet. The following morning the text of journeys appear on snow: trident marks of pheasant, double slots of fallow deer, dabs of rabbit. When it thaws, slush trickles into drains taking the journal of that night with it. Yellow wallflowers begin to rouse.

Marsh marigold

Water comes to this dark place out of sorrow. In
the pool under broken alders, a chieftain of the Old
North was killed in battle and his head carried on a
stick away from where Tern meets Severn to high
ground in the west. 'Usual is the wind from the
east,' usual for a proud man and a thrush among
thorns and the outcry against oppression, 'usual
for crows to find flesh in a nook.'* Unusual is gold
fallen in mud to rise into the air and, through the
river fog, sing for our eyes.

* Llewarch Hen, 'Usual is the Wind', *Red Book of Hergest VI*
(sixth century).

Dandelion

Bold as brass, a dandelion bursts from the muddy,
dog-peed path. Out from a dark winter place,
rudely sunny, a kind of memorial sprouts from the
top of its lion-tooth root which stretches all the
way down to Australia. A green knot peels and a
gold cone opens its fingers. The solar disk, with rays
yellow as a wax crayon drawing, when looked at
closely is an astronomical image of the sun in all its
boiling flaring power, firing atomic storms across
the poles.

One day of warm sunshine and the dandelion
flower is an entire landscape, a piss-a-bed daystar
around which other planets orbit. In trees above, a
song thrush oils his tunes, not quite ready yet but
his creaky phrases mean something wonderful to all
who hear them. Even the pushing-shoving jackdaws
leave the thrush alone, out on a limb, lost in
exultant reverie. A couple of robins and a coven of
long-tailed tits pass through the trees and their calls
and early songlines are clear as chrome but nowhere
near the pitch and intensity of the thrush. Buzzards

and ravens pass with only sideways comment.

All of a sudden it's warm enough and bright
enough to believe in the dandelion. There is a fly
that does, too. As if conjured from the squalor of
the path and drawn in by the flower's gravity, the
fly fastens to its brassy rays searching for liquid
gold. It is softly and almost transparently jewel-like
with *art nouveau* window-paned wings, bristling
with sensors and both delicate and powerful. From
a distance the fly seems just a blemish on the
flower but for the dandelion it is the reason for its
explosion of life. This is an ephemeral solar system.
Once pollinated by the fly the flower will turn into
a clock, to blow away on solar winds.

Wood spurge

Under the knobbly dark of alders the brook bites
into soft tissue below roots and spits a little beach
into the crook of its curve. There, a handful of
shale beads each holed through by bitter spurge
sap, milk of enmity. Above the trees, a half-turn
cut of the moon's bloody cipher hangs and sharp-
footed spoor sign the streamside where we, the
enemy, baptise our princesses.

Skunk cabbage

I bit into the spadix, the flower neck inside the
yellow hood of the spathe, when the Horse Pool
was drained. It was just after the fish were stunned
by jump-leads from a big truck battery and scooped
up, silvery and bog-eyed, from the surface before
the water went down the sluice. We kept a few
pike back and they circled each other like knifemen
in a spring-fed tank in the woods. We ate one of
them: its white flesh tasted as dark and muddy as
Hughey's hanky which he wiped his hands with,
angry that this pool-dredging business was so dirty.
The rest of us were covered in shit for weeks.

When I looked at the big cabbagey paddle leaves
with lemon-yellow arum flowers of skunk cabbage
reflected in the pool of floating fish, I wondered
if this was suddenly an edible landscape. All we
had to do was eat what had been presented to us;
we could survive on what we saw now that it had
been conjured from a world which had been hiding
all along inside the everyday one we were used
to. This was ancestral hunter-gathering. So, I bit

into the spadix. It was a couple of seconds before I realised my mistake. At first the celery-crunch felt good but after an instant a sense of yellowness, maybe mustard gas, leaked from the bite and my mouth was cauterised – not like chilli, more like boiling ink. I floundered around gasping, a fish out of water, mouth burning, eyes watering; this edible world was a cruelly toxic deception.

When the water drained I saw mud – dark, fluid, dangerous slop – as if it were the sump of our reality. It stank, somewhere between skunk – which has a kind of polecatty musk mixed with thiol molecules of sulphurous rubber egg – and archaeology. Down where the skunk cabbage punched its fat white taproot was a drowned horse (after which the pool was named), coot eggs, fish bones, beer bottles, a lady's shoe, a missing knife, sedge pollen, rusty nails, alder leaves, bricks from a demolished house – a couple of centuries-worth of wonders. Without thinking, I had bitten the flowering end of what the root was growing in and now all that stuff was on fire in my mouth. The history of the Horse Pool and those of us who worked there came through the stink of mud and taste of skunk cabbage.

Big yellow machines arrived that spring, dug out all the crap; the pool filled up with water again and we launched the three surviving pike.

Flag iris

She is something, nonetheless. The way an oak
grows, a frog swims, a swallow flies, a spring
oozes, a wind blows, every spasm of an earthly
love and each accident of malice and error thirsts
for appreciation but in this muddy pond, nothing
answers. A bird-woman in the dawn sky, her
hand draped across her crouching knee, her wings
folded behind her back, golden, with a halo. She
looks down on yellow irises and feels optimistic,
lucky even.

Daffodil

Down in Dymock, on the red clay of Severn Vale,
the daffodils packed in boxes went to London on
the train and poets went to War. Neither came
back. They say a shell passed so close to Edward
Thomas's heart it stopped. When he walked the
yellow wood* did he ever have an inkling such a
thing could happen, that the power of something
passing could kill you? Don't stand too close to
the railway line or step beyond the daffodils at
wood's edge.

* 'Two roads diverged in a yellow wood / And sorry I could
not travel both,' Robert Frost, 'The Road Not Taken' (1916).

Bees on wild carrot

White

Snowdrop

The eye is drawn to white from far off, a dinner-plate-sized clump on a bend in the brook. Whiter than swans on the river; whiter than snow on the Stiperstones; whiter than lines on the road or polypropylene sacks of asbestos fly-tipped in the wood – there is something both vestal and venal about snowdrops. Flowering moon-white for the purity of milk in time for Candlemas and Imbolc, these were not planted by anyone but washed down in a flood years ago. Bulbous with religious symbolism and feelings for the coming spring, snowdrops also have a stubborn streak. There is something belligerent in their timing. There is joy in the reassurance of snowdrops for a world which has lost so many seasonal signatures but there is also something mechanically insistent, perfunctory and routine which corrupts their beauty, too. Looking closely at the flowers, perhaps it's the vividness of green dots and dashes in them which transcends both vestal and venal to become vernal. Too much whiteness blinds and I almost miss the

black backpack lying next to the snowdrops by the
brook. Inside it is a mess of damp clothes, a little
purse of small change and a couple of bank cards.
The bag feels heavy with stories, secrets, worries:
how it got there, who it belongs to, what to do
with it. As I climb up the bank from the brook,
holding the bag, my eye is drawn back through
all the winter-washed brown-green-greys, back to
the patch of white. It's a colour as shrill as the cry
the tawny owl makes cornered by jays. Whatever
strange or sinister thing happened here, the
snowdrops remain implacable.

Sweet violet

One night the beast has a premonition. He smells the abattoir on the breeze, crashes the fence and makes it into the wood. When I find him he is hiding in brambles, as big as a train, a honeyed leather colour with peat-pool eyes. Farmer is out searching but I won't grass him up. The next day he's gone, leaving only a patch of white violets. I've seen him since, charging over western hills with the sunset in his horns, stamping under frosty trees, snorting the breath of spring. He is the one who understands life and wherever he goes there will be freedom.

Lily-of-the-valley

What was in your bridal bunch on Walpurgis
Night? Flowers which grew down the stony wood
and in the dark behind the shed, that chippies
hid in rooftops, that witches brewed a toxic
fragrance from (still illegal in some countries),
and a tonic for cardiac arrhythmia and the
melancholy, plucked from white-lady footsteps of
the Bohemian Virgin, a gift of life in that terrible
valley which runs from your house all the way to
the thunderer's sister.*

* In Old Germanic custom, lily-of-the-valley was dedicated to
Osara, goddess of spring and sister of Thor.

Toothwort

It must be fifty years since a train passed along the
old railway line. A breeze bringing new weather
raced in from the south-west holding the promise
of rain in its teeth but, like a dog with a stick,
wouldn't drop it and kept on running. From the
abandoned railway line, which was now a broad
path through the woods, he looked out between
trees across fields at the foot of Wenlock Edge
and strained to hear the cuckoo. The sound of
birds from the woods was intense. Even though
he was listening to one small stretch of woodland,
perhaps half a mile long, this was only a section
of a continuous ribbon of trees which ran for 20
miles. The breeze was clearing the dust glued to
warm air, sweeping over the woods, gathering
birdsong. The birds, ecstatic with their own songs
and buoyed by the collective power of all the
other singers around them, were delirious. From
where he stood, the woods were like speakers
from which came anarchic music, amplified by the
breeze flowing into and along the Edge. Inside the

woods, the crackling energy which gave voice to birdsong was also surging through the vegetation. Wood sorrel, sanicle, yellow archangel, herb Paris, early purple orchid; bluebells with their narcotic scent swirling under leafing trees; wild garlic bursting into a constellation of stars. In amongst all this was a plant of toothwort, a strange pigment-less parasite of tree roots whose ghostly translucent white stems with small yellow and pink flowers emerged from the earth bringing a note of mysterious stillness. The toothwort, also called corpse flower, reminded him of something else.

There had been so much rain and the leaves were almost umbrella'd out so the humidity was trapped in a thick almost aquatic green light. Striking through the landscape were bright slashes of oil-seed rape fields. They were subsidy yellow – a dazzling colour, sickly sweet with the scent of public money extravagantly poured into the countryside to reduce its wildlife and maximise profits, a corporate colour running counter to the white pulse of spring coursing through the flowering May, wild garlic, cow parsley, stitchwort, jack-by-the-hedge. Up on the steep slopes of Edge Wood, the wild garlic was just about peaking. The canopy of trees had now closed over the great, almost vertical lawns of white flower and the sexy, animal-like musk from their leaves. Inside the woods, deer and small birds stirred the white-on-green heraldry.

He, an anonymous nutter in the woods, was drowned out by the songs of chiffchaff, blackcap, redstart and garden warblers; orchard blossom, wood anemone and stitchwort; high blue skies zipping with swallows. Spring emerged within the traditional timings of events such as migrant bird arrivals, frog spawn and leaf opening, unlike many previous years when it all went askew. Was this a return to a seasonal rhythm he thought had been lost or was it a seasonal aberrancy? Time would tell.

The oak leaves were out before the ash, which meant he was going to have a splash instead of a soak, the norm for the last couple of years when ash leafed before oak. This year the omens were good, at least for the weather. Leaves were loaded with omen; auguries and symbols opened within spring flowers. As bluebells and wild garlic flowered in the woods, there seemed a greater feeling that spring of what the Germans call *Stimmung* – something like sentiment, mood, an emotive state which tuned the soul to Nature. There, in green woods with corpse flowers, the rain brought a quickening as spring careered over hills and woods passed May Day.

Poet's narcissus

Beneath the trees, they nod indolently like a flock
of little blind gulls with their beaks open. The
suffering the rest of us go through gives them
something to squawk about. God moves among
them, His word rattling around His mouth like
a brick in a concrete mixer – *quand même*, the
word is, 'nonetheless'. They begin shaking their
wings, desperate to lift into the wind but they're
anchored underground, straining until they
explode in a burst of pillow down – a victory of
beautiful but pointless innocence, nonetheless.
'Vicious bastards with suspicious stains on their
trousers,' that's Jim's verdict on poets.

Petunia

A windy day in Flanders: a sharp westerly ripples the moat of a small chateau with trim lawns and box hedges framing the gate house full of fine furniture and *objets d'art*. Beyond the wrought-iron balustrade, trees vanish into a wide sweep of country far away. On the terrace are dark-green wooden boxes filled with white petunias. These flowers are not quite right for this place, not quite what is needed, like an error the eye is drawn to.

Not too far from the chateau are the tidy, regimented cemeteries for those who fell in the Great War, including my grandfather's two brothers, out there somewhere in a pit of lime. Back home, their names are on a war memorial next to the Iron Bridge. Unlike the wild red poppies which burst from dormant seeds woken up by battle, the floral decorations for cemeteries and memorials are the same across Europe – open, innocent petunias, planted to be ripped up and dumped; temporary, slight – not quite what is needed, like a mistake.

According to Russell Page in *The Education of a Gardener* (1962), 'Any feebleness of idea in design or in planting will, because the foreground is weak, only bring the background into prominence.'

Mossy saxifrage

A dangerous desire is loose in the undiscovered world. Only the wind pronounces the love it stole from wet, dripping crags. Only small white flowers in the scree sing of devotion. Only bog-muck swallowing the jealous years of rain whispers promises. You stand, in the lightning of nameless passion the mountains stand. Behind you, a bag full of unspeakable memories.

Wild garlic

In the manner of stars, they flower and stink. In
spring's midnight, under smouldering heavens and
leafless ash, there is a whining above them: little
grey hoverflies* crying over spilt milk.

* *Portevinia maculata*

Crambe

Morris amongst the gladioli: straightens his back,
eyes grown accustomed to peering into soil squint
now over 'long fields'* to the other side of the
valley where he's from. Morris is too big for the
flowerbed, his hands like five pounds of sausages
let go the spade handle and fall limp at his sides.
His ears, as if chewed by caterpillars, pick up the
thrush knocking a snail shell on the wall-top, the
whisper of a grass snake through the box hedge
and something threading its way along the breeze
to knot into the tie he wears even on a day like
this. Morris is listening, remembering something
rising from the clod under his boots. Before he has
a chance to register what that is, we mob him like
jays round an owl. Led as usual by Terence, those
of us who get the joke point to Morris's hat and
mutter something about a foot poking out, an ear,
a tail. He's confused at first, shaken from a quiet
moment in the flowers and laughs along with it.

* The Welsh *hiraeth* – homesickness, a melancholy longing for
the old place – literally translated as 'long field'.

But Scouse Terry – who was once a navy gunner and witness to an atomic bomb going off on Bikini atoll – is goading him, worming into Morris's psyche like he's worming his way into Morris's family. Morris becomes increasingly vexed that we can see a rabbit hiding under the old cloth cap he always wears. He snatches the hat off his head and looks inside it, not knowing that what he's planting will grow big and coarse and blurt into laughing sprays of white flowers long after he's gone. And not knowing that one day quite soon we will dance on Terence's grave. 'If you bastards have put anything in my bloody hat,' shouts Morris, 'I'll bloody swing for the lot of you!'

Ox-eye daisy

He drove this way a long time ago, on the Roman
road which linked remote parts of the Empire. She
sat beside him, with her son in the back seat of the
big old Humber, and she twitched and mumbled,
clutching a bunch of moon daisies, dog daisies, ox-
eye daisies, (same difference). He can't remember
now why but he had a responsibility to get the
boy's poor mad mother to a place of safety. She
kept shoving the flowers in his face as if he must
acknowledge them, see and smell them to know
what she knew about the spell or curse the howling
daisies held but she couldn't say it in words. He
had to keep pushing her hand away so he could see
the road.

Newly widened, the road now cuts across the
lie of the land, its banks planted for magpies and
plastic. All the way from an archipelago of mini-
roundabouts to the Snack Van lay-by, ten thousand
ox-eyes watch the vroom of traffic. British daisies
open skyward, cheerfully gormless, but these bend
their gaze to the ground because they are a Balkan

subspecies of the vulgar *Leucanthemum* picked for the lycanthrope: white flowers for Olga the Werewolf.

Loose clouds, cables strung across the plain and the road all travel east. A skylark lands on a fence post and another, a stone's throw away, climbs into the sky, singing. Skipper butterflies feed on gold. A ditch running from the fields under the road carries the dark slick of an ancient marsh. A lost village hides under the mound of trees. Other secrets – the cremation cemetery, the stone-blade place and Gallows Nooking – have been re-abandoned under ash and poplar roots. Life is ploughed out of the rest of this landscape and any return is forbidden.

In the lay-by, Olga plucks at the white paper napkin wrapping a sausage sandwich – 'Воли ме . . . не воли ме'*. She stares from the Snack Van's hatch at the moon rising above an embankment of moon daisies, dog daisies, ox-eye daisies, the songs of skylarks passing into a relentless forever.

* Serbian, 'he loves me. . . he loves me not.'

cyclamens
seacroft

Pink

Pyramidal orchid

One day They will pay a hangman to take these
beautiful souls. Orchids flower on the windy hill,
butterflies and moths fly over the grass and a
kestrel takes to the sky from a ruined stone tower
screaming the beloved's name, a shadow which
cuts across the meadow like a scythe. They (you
know Them?) walk there and They walk here. A
summer gale has blown sticks out of linden trees,
strewing paths along the river where cold brown
cables of rain haul life in and drag life away. They
walk where We, (1) kiss under cherry trees and,
(2) huddle around a box of sandwiches in park
shelters. The noose, through which these years
slip, hangs from the bridge.

Turtlehead

It was somewhere in Illinois. The car pulled up
above a gulley and he walked down towards
the stream where it went through a pipe.
Along there was a rose turtlehead: a pink face
withdrawn from the ululating grey of old railroad
land, into a lost prairie memory. Locomotive,
bison, mustang. . . these things had slowed
right down to a stop inside the shell of a flower
thrown up by the stream which ran out of loess
bluffs beyond. This tallgrass territory, like pulp
Westerns in a junk box, was a rubbed-out kind
of place. He crouched listening to the turtlehead
under an overcast sky, not daring to raise his
profile above the gulley in case of stray bullets.
She whispered Chelone's curse: how the prairie
creatures, such as passenger pigeons, were invited
to God's stupid wedding but she refused to
leave home and for that she was condemned to
wear her little rosy shack like a tortoise and to
suffer in silence forever; the prairie creatures,
like passenger pigeons, never came back. She

told him to get in his car and drive through the dust of Illinois' dirt roads and listen to country stations on the radio – all those goddamn songs were about her.

Common centaury

The dead – spectres of guilt, weedy bestowers
of a profound grace – find you in a dream. They
chose you and you throw up glass. Now you brush
flowers from your hair – centuary, storksbill,
pyramidal orchid, mallow – which fall onto a
grassy hill where moths fasten on their sweetness.
This 'now' you're dreaming comes without the
permanence the dead have planned for you;
instead summer breathes in your face.

Musk mallow

Little Doll-face smiles in Babylon: before this
patch of scrub between the roadside and the wood
became abandoned, it was a builder's yard with
piles of roof tiles, galvanised sheeting, drainpipes,
house bricks. Before then it was the town tip
where lorry loads of rubbish were dumped and
crushed until the hole overflowed. Before then
it was a quarry pit where stone was blown and
broken, lugged to kilns and burnt into lime for
smelting iron. Before then it was a cave picked
out of the rock into the darkness of the Great
Mystery, Mother of Harlots and all Disgusting
Things of the Earth. Broken into by the quarry,
stuffed full of the town's shite, abandoned by the
builder, She slinked off into the woods. There's a
time and a place for everything, Little Doll-face,
and before Her Beast locks onto your loveliness,
you are free in the ruins of this country.

Sainfoin

I could see the flower through the clear pane in the old gas bill envelope which landed on my doormat. The scribbled note on the back said it was Sainfoin. Like a tiny pink lupin with vetch-like pinnate leaves, this pea relative is said to have been introduced from France where it was called 'St Foyn' in the seventeenth century. As a fodder crop, Sanfoin was so nourishing to cattle it was called 'Holy Hay' – 'sain' meaning sound or healthy and 'foin' meaning hay.

Opening the envelope and taking out the flower was to open a history of this countryside which has largely been lost. The Sainfoin became an emblem of those traditional flower-rich hay meadows which once covered much of this landscape. Only in relict or protected fields, strips of roadside verge and odd corners where the grass has not been 'improved' by chemical fertiliser and herbicide, do the hay flowers survive.

In these hot June days, meadow brown and ringlet butterflies, together with six-spot burnet moths, bumblebees, solitary bees and hoverflies visit other pea family plants: bird's-foot trefoils, melilots, medicks, vetches and clovers. These plants were once staples of livestock diet and supported a wide range of insects too, and their beautiful flowers of pink, blue, yellow and white tell a story of agricultural experiment and abandoned ideas. Many of the plant species in fodder crops were introduced from Europe or other parts of the world. Varieties were selected from native and introduced species for specific qualities or adaption to specific soils; they hang on in a very changed world.

As I wander the places where these flowers grow it seems to me that the plants that once fed animals, which then fed people, have still got an important role in our lives – it's not just bodies that need nourishment. I track down the Holy Hay to the edge of a copse where someone long ago chucked Sainfoin seeds down for their cows not knowing that three hundred years later we would value the flowers like rare jewels, a living, vernacular treasure.

Incarvillia

After centuries of skirmishes, sieges, occupation
and counter-insurgency, there had to be an
end to slaughter in the outlands. There was no
complete cessation of violence – men still roared
like bulls at each other in pub car parks – but
peace did come, slowly. It was not what it looked
like. The garden grew from bones, clay and the
cold ashes of beacons under castle walls once
red with blood and black with crows. Wandering
immortals ground up the dawn to make the
colours of flowers but the clouds were tinged
with grief so when they bloomed the garden
rang with joy and sadness at the same time. A
particular flower caused a stir when it turned
up under lead wyverns on the gate pillars in the
Fountain Garden. We were told it was called
Incarvillia in honour of Pierre Nicholas Le Chéron
d'Incarville, a Jesuit explorer and diplomat
who died in Peking in 1757 failing to convert
Emperor Qianlong but passing his ponsey French
name on to plants which seemed at odds with

the defence and propagation of his faith. The *Incarvillia* or False Gloxinia or Chinese trumpet in the Fountain Garden carried the name of its European discoverer, too. *Incarvillia delavayii* was also named after Père Jean Marie Delavay, another Jesuit missionary who walked alone in the mountains of Yunnan stealing the most wonderful plants and sending them back to Europe until he died slowly of bubonic plague in 1895. We liked the name, 'Chinese trumpet'. The *suo-na*, Chinese trumpet, is an instrument of the common people. It has a double reed and tiny bell to make notes we hadn't heard before, like crane song to chase away evil; celebrate funerals and weddings. To our ears the *suo-na* sounded like wasps. We were always having run-ins with wasps. One day, Brian was out in the Wilderness cutting grass with a strimmer when he accidentally weed-whacked a wasps' nest. They all buzzed through a split in his pants and stung him on the bollocks; he swelled up like a trumpet. Robert went to Brian's aid but the wasps stung him too so he drove home to fetch his shotgun, came back, walked up to the wasps' nest in the Wilderness and, ka-boom! Both barrels. We half-heard the fountain's gush and gurgle – depending on how the stopcock was set – as we busied around flower borders in the shade of clipped yew hedges. In the outlands, our gardens concealed their terrible violences under an imperial orderliness. We marvelled at this simple Buddha-tuber from the mountains of the Far East which pushed out choice ferny leaves and trumpet flowers with such a meeting of glee and sorrow that its history and ours cancelled each other out. Far from mist-gathered mountains opening on Tibet, we looked east from the Fountain Garden's wyvern gate towards the green hills of the Welsh Marches and this flower was pinker than knickers on a washing line.

Sweet William

Poor Billy, when he sniffed her scent on the
breeze from the cypress trees and got a nosebleed,
he should've shut up. But instead he sang those
fearless Maoist songs about how the dying sun
looked like blood and how a thousand mountains
were waiting for our leisure because he thought
she was ardent. Bill? Everyone else was too busy
dividing up the land to notice she had danced
away with his eyes and stuffed his sockets with
small-time whore carnations.

Restharrow

I've hit a snag, she said as her knees buckled,
ropes to her shoulder-yoke snapped taut then
sagged and she sank to the ground in front of the
sprung iron bed frame she was dragging across the
hill. Prostrate, face down, pointing east towards
sunrise, she stared into the turf: rabbit droppings,
a thicket of intestinal leaves, tiny black springtails,
a red worm, a grasshopper, bare earth with
limestone fragments concealing the snare of roots.
I do God's work, she cried but God's foot pressed
into the small of her back. Dawn and sunset
flushed her cheeks where she lay until nightfall.

Phlox Spitfire

It's all about the smell: the grass on the hill was tinder dry that summer. Crickets and grasshoppers fiddled fast enough for sparks to fly and set the hill alight. A half-drunk flagon of cider, stopper undone, lay on sheep-scuffed earth under a hawthorn twisted by winds and the only shade for half a mile. Lovers buttoned, resting against the tree trunk, lighting cigarettes, swigging from the bottle and laughing. Swallows flew high above the hill in a hazy sky as dark clouds began to heave over the horizon. Suddenly, the roar of an engine scared linnets from the tree. The lovers looked up into the face of the machine-animal which had picked up an immortal scent from the embers of their bodies. That smell.

Cyclamen

Their name comes from the Latin *cyclaminos*
and the Greek *kuklos*, meaning circle. Their
story comes from warm dry forests of the
Mediterranean. Their colour comes from an
enduring optimism and an innocence of spirit
toughing it out here in the woods. The cyclamen,
much smaller than the showy, potted ones in the
grocers, have been in Britain since the sixteenth
century – and in this wood for about a hundred
years. They belong to the primrose family, which
accounts for their irrepressible cheeriness, a
pink note they strike at the end instead of the
beginning of the year. When I first found them
about twenty years ago in the far corner of this
little wood once used as a quarry for limekilns, the
cyclamen were a single clump the size of a saucer.
Since then, shaded by ash trees and hawthorns,
their ivy-like leaves struggled through a thickening
carpet of real ivy. That saucer-sized clump
expanded into a coffee-table-sized patch then,
as it spread further, separated out into smaller

pink dinner-plate islands in an ocean of glossy green. The quarry and the house next to it were abandoned a hundred years ago. Only the relics of a garden remain: a few conifers, some flowering currant bushes and the cyclamen. I imagine the story of this patch began with a handful of tiny corms from a bulb catalogue, planted to pop up pink each summer. Those corms rolled out from a long history. Cyclamen were grown in the medieval gardens of Constantinople because they appeared so different from common flowers of the fields. The flower's circular 'eye', formed by the fusing of upswept petals, peers earthward like a microscope. Its pink flushed with purple draws the human eye, especially in a season of grey skies and brown rot. Its evergreen, grey-enamelled leaves have neatness and precision. Now the cyclamen seem to belong here as much as the ash trees and, in these anxious shadows, may outlive them.

Artichoke

Blue

Monk's-hood

The wet from Valais snow-melt and rain flowed
down alpine meadows and just before it trickled
into the stream by the cabin it licked the clump
of monk's-hood. Hooded, helmeted flower
contraptions of sprung lids, blue as an old police
box, they signalled the presence of *Aconitum*, a
notorious poison of wives and wolves. In that
stone cabin with a scythe hanging from the
ceiling, the sorcerer read a Persian text* and went
in search of the mouse immune to monk's-hood,
a theriac to use as an antidote. Too late; the
neurotoxin unlocked a path which led him from
the sky deep into the mountain where there were
others huddled on a corner, hoods up against
CCTV cameras.

* Guy de Vigevani (1335) wrote of the archive of a
Persian scholar, Avicenna or Ibn Sina (980–1037), which
recommended searching for the mouse antidote to *Aconitum*
poisoning. From De Cleene and Lejeune, *Compendium of
Symbolic and Ritual Plants of Europe* (2003).

Forget-me-not

These are the last dark days before the end. These are the days of butterflies. The sound is a grind of jawbones clogged with earwax, the drone of bees and traffic far off. The smell is a desperate fragrance of April gardens through which butterflies roar above the shouts and tears of a family break-up, their blue wings flashing with the insignia of extinction.

Nettle-leaved bellflower

Where the sun rolls the nipple of the grassy hill,
thin green wires coil blonde stems to suspend a
cradle of sharp blue instruments. A fat-hoofed
clockhorse clomps seconds from the stone-ridged
path up to the top and a pissy juice of years
leaches down to feed the bumblebee traps of
bellflowers below. Bordello black and scarlet,
six-spot burnet moths swing on the nodding idiot
scabious flower through a lavender-blue sky and
deep, deep under roots, the fossilised fury of
the mollusc's empire heaves. This heart-shaped
piece of ground is thrown to the birds and every
morning two crows peck the truth out of it.

Delphinium Pacific Giant

The border ran all along a high redbrick wall the
length of the croquet lawn. Its soil was bastard-
trenched and mucked. Tallest at the back, shortest
at the front, they were planted in threes, fives or
sevens in variety. Mulched with a year's worth
of dark fermented compost from a heap where
grass snakes incubated eggs and bottles of tea
kept warm in winter; staked with inch-and-a-half
square larch and tied by sisal twine smelling of
dry sheds; they grew tall and lush until they filled
the entire space and their flower spikes reached
head-height. St John's fire lit the blue touchpaper:
flashes of cobalt, sky, cerulean, azure, lapis,
midnight, electrified the border. Neptune waded
through the delphiniums. Shark-eyed, kelp-
bearded in his admiral's hat, dragging eels and
anchors, his wavelength passed in a blue aurora
along the wall, his shadow slopping bilge across
the croquet lawn. Ol' Tune it was who made these
flowers from a dolphin. A miracle: the dolphin
rescued a man from drowning and after hearing

his story, a mob went in search of the dolphin;
so to protect her, the sea god turned her into a
flower with dolphin-shaped nectaries and the
Romans called her *Delphinium*. Now her seeds are
thrown into the solstice flames of midsummer to,
'dispel darkness in the sight and strengthen one's
power of seeing.'* Look into the delphiniums: the
deep ocean swells around island cliffs.

* Ortus Sanitatis (1485), in De Cleene and Lejeune,
Compendium of Symbolic and Ritual Plants of Europe (2003).

Pansy

A bed of pansies tilts flat blue faces to the sun like
a deaf and dumb funeral. All you can hear is the
rustle of sleeves as signers argue at the graveside
and scuff gravel on the path. Whoever lies in the
coffin is leaving an angry silence. Stepping back, as
if listening to this is an intrusion, I go for a break,
frustrated anyway at lifting sods with a turfing
iron. When I come back the funeral is over. The
mourners have quietly slipped away. The pansies
are rotating their dials further west. I go to fetch
my leather jacket from where I've left it on the
grass behind some headstones and there's a garden
fork stuck through it.

Sea pea

The first lighthouse on Orford Ness, built in 1792, was known as an occulting lighthouse because it had a dark area created by a blanked-out section of the glass top which broke the rotating light beam. Occulting is an appropriate term for this dark, mysterious space in the most marginal of lands and one of the UK's most important and most secretive military establishments where the darkest arts of war were practiced.

Keep to the old military concrete roads. There are still unexploded munitions, chunks of TNT; the shingle itself is dangerous. Although the wind is relentless, bright sunshine has heated the stones and a haze shimmers over the shingle. Like apparitions flickering in the kind of arid landscape seen in war zones on the news, the Pagodas rise from the stones. Six huge concrete buildings the size of cathedrals, their strange architecture hunched under shoulders of shingle obscure their outline. Some have had their aluminium roofs picked clean to their skeletons, some squat like malign bunkers, others have massive concrete roofs suspended on pillars which have given rise to the name Pagoda – houses of worship where sacred relics are stored for veneration, spiritually charged places which draw the lightning. The sacred relics these Pagodas once housed were atomic bombs.

From the Atomic Weapons Research Establishment in 1953 and throughout the Cold War, these massive laboratories on Orford Ness tested every conceivable combination of physical situation and stress which nuclear weapons may be subject to without exploding before the appointed moment. They don't look like laboratories.

Footsteps on bright stones alarm rock doves which clatter out of the darkness entering a Pagoda called Lab Five. As eyes become accustomed, the brain struggles to make sense of the place: twisted metal suspended in deadened space; an Escher-like complex of balconies connected by steps down to a deep and sinister pit; cruciform shapes on the wall and a fresco of numbers, calibrated in feet and metres.

The silence holds a vibration – a ghostly aural image of some terrible, cataclysmic noise. This is not the temple of an unknown civilisation and the only thing that makes sense is its dereliction.

Now these Pagodas crumble as if the secrets they held are on self-destruct, reducing them slowly to the stones on which they stand. But the shingle offers no sense of security, walk on the steep slope down to the sea – it shifts and slides underfoot, drawing and exhausting energy into its flow. On ridges by the sea, near the flat, flotsam nests of lesser black-backed gulls, sea kale and sea pea – plants which have sustained people in the past – grow out of the shingle. The sea pea was first recorded in Britain in 1575 at Orford Ness and is said to have once saved the local community from famine. Botanists claimed the sea pea was poisonous to save this rare and exclusive shingle plant from exploitation – a little story put about to keep a secret.

Lab One, next to heaps of tangled metal and the thing that looks like a bus stop where they used to serve tea. The padlocked door clanks open. Step inside the cool white chamber. The echoes are too loud to talk, too loud almost for thoughts. Here, lying in state, is WE177A. Reach out to touch the cold metal, at a loss to know how to respond to it. It's 2.8 m long, 42 cm in diameter and weighs 272 kg. It's a classic bomb-shape with fins and pointed nose cone; off-white with the orange band denoting a British nuclear weapon; a yellow band which warns of high explosives and a little brown rectangle which means who-knows-what. Its serial numbers reveal it's a tactical nuclear gravity bomb to be dropped from a plane. It has a variable yield from 20 to 200 kt – that's twenty times more powerful than the bombs dropped on Hiroshima. Here it lies, decommissioned, withdrawn from service in 1998.

Melancholy thistle

The softest kiss lies buried in the thistle. Listening
to gutters choked with rain, pouring on a world
we no longer believe in. Did we ever believe? We
reach for each other and hear the fall of hooves as
Long Mynd ponies, tails bannering the west wind,
gallop across the hills towards extinction.

Wild thyme

A ginger-bottomed bumblebee in wild thyme –
there's a sight redolent of a pastoral landscape
as rich in stories of myth and magic and drama
as the soil which sustains it. Purple thyme and
knapweed, yellow lady's bedstraw and St John's
Wort and white eyebright are inhabited by
bees, bumblebees, hoverflies and butterflies in
a dreamlike tale of this land as powerful as any
line from Shakespeare. 'I know a bank where
the wild thyme blows,' says Oberon to Puck the
wanderer of *A Midsummer Night's Dream*. This is
a landscape which, like the bumblebee foraging
for nectar, draws those in search of a good story.

On the weekend of the storytelling festival on
Wenlock Edge, a shanty of marquees and stages
seemed to belong to a culture which owed as
much to the 1560s as it did to the 1960s. Even
though the equipment was new and the ways
of speaking them were based on even newer
experience and imagination, many of the stories
the storytellers brought were as old as the hills, or

at least old as the people who ever wandered the hills. From around the world, stories which seeped out of creation myths, stowed away in shipping trunks, ran from the dusty pages of parish registers and mythologies with their bags of beans and impossible quests to turn up in a pub somewhere, turned up here.

The sky cleared for a couple of days and real sunshine made the experience more unreal. In a night of music, ale and honeysuckle shadows, people reinvented themselves as characters in story. All the stories were drawn up by the grass and trees and midsummer spaces rolling over the Edge; drawn up in a dreaminess of bees in the wild thyme of Nature's telling.

Dahlia Trelissick Purple

Unwrapped, the tubers looked like feet. We stood
it at the back of the border in the corner by the
steps and gave it plenty of compost. When it grew
I had to use eight-foot stakes to tie the stems and
when it flowered, ten feet tall, we were in awe of
Mictecacihuatl's* lantern-blooms and could hear *los
Angelitos* of the Yucatan midnight.

* Aztec goddess of death and queen of the underworld.

Harebell

Blue on blue: harebells on the hill against a bright-blue sky, the autumn equinox was a day of dazzling clarity, a tiny moment of balance. Who was to know that the storm which rages now would come out of the blue. Around that perfect note of bell-like sunshine was plenty of chaos. Jays screeched on edge through the wood like fingernails on blackboards. Grey squirrels raced around tree trunks and across hazel tops, hyped up on sex 'n' nuts 'n' rock 'n' roll. Chittering and skrawking, the jays and squirrels were driven by that autumnal creative spirit. It was this same spirit which lured me in search of the source of the River Clun in the liminal lands of the west. The river's source, that most fugitive of ideas, was fastened to the hills at Anchor, the furthest west village in Shropshire. Up in the Clun Forest, hard against the Welsh border and with one of the best unspoiled pubs in the Marches, a colony of house martins or pub martins, dived into their teapots under the eaves, feeding a late brood.

What was once called the Swan Pool behind the pub and the official source, was drained into boggy fields in the 1970s and the real origin was Bettws Wood, a hill of conifer plantation over relict patches of moorland and bog. Pull a hank of bright-green sphagnum moss from the track's gutter and squeeze it and that could easily claim to be the source of the river. Red kite, raven, stonechat, peacock butterfly, take to the still blue air in this high place apart. Neither England nor Wales, on the turn, halfway between light and dark, where a river begins as rumour this place has such liminal energy. Now ditched, the trickle from Bettws Wood collected in a puddle brown as cake, cornered by the road and flowed proper, with the name of the Clun, eastwards into England where the first storm of autumn found us the next day still drowsy from the blues.

Brown

Lady's bedstraw

It may have a been a day like this – grey above and gold below with a fresh breeze stirring leaves and something in the land which should've been left alone. Down in Corve Dale, jays clattered from oak trees fat with acorns as hunters with a pack of hounds splashed through the River Corve hunting mink, as they once hunted otters here. Buzzards idled round the sky and even sparring ravens couldn't dislodge their careful circles. A sparrow hawk found itself in a mob of house martins. This gathering time before the trip south gets the martins agitated and they took against the hawk without touching it.

Higher still on Edge top, a few wild cherries burned scarlet against the greys of rock face and low cloud. From the scraped-flat quarry floor and its derelict iron machines lying like abandoned sarcophagi, a thin pathway snaked across the stone bank, up over the lip of the hole and away. This path, untrodden by human feet, crossed a scrap of land where a few butterflies, dragonflies and knapweed flowers soaked up a rare ray of sunlight. This was all that remained of Westwood Common, a once large stretch of open limestone grassland on the Edge, almost completely obliterated by quarrying since the middle of the last century.

It may have been on such a day that Nanny Morgan walked the common for the last time, along a path like this through lady's bedstraw, its fragrance lost to memory like a sweet but malicious rumour. A great beauty it was said but evil it was said, too; she lived on the common in a house called Five Chimneys. Feared by local people but paid for spells and curses by them, Nanny Morgan the witch was murdered here in September 1857 on a day like this – grey above and gold below, with a breeze stirring something best left alone now.

Broad bean

Like a derelict telephone exchange, the stalks
shrivel on their sticks, losing the connection
between earth and sky. Their flowers, called
'letters of mourning', are now shelled pods
leaving bean-money, funding an old death cult.
They rattle in the bag and spill onto gambling
tables to be counted. A jam jar, a roll of blotting
paper, a splash of water and a soul emerges like
ectoplasm – testa, root hair, cotyledon (remember
the diagram?) – professors, market traders,
receptionists, drivers – they're all sprouting on
windowsills, waiting for Epiphany.

Ground-elder

Open the soil where white rhizomes thread through holes as small as worm heads into a torpid entanglement of other roots. In winter there's nothing to spray with systemic herbicide or cover in black polythene, it's gone underground. Dig it all up. With forensic diligence, pick every last piece, even a few cells left in the rootball of another plant is enough to restart this pernicious nightmare.

It's dusk, as always. His car is parked at the far end of the car park. He walks towards it carrying a toolbox and a shovel as an old pickup arcs round and stops in front of him. Two men get out, late thirties, never seen them before but they look like trouble. They ask questions, threateningly; there are no answers, just more intimidation. It's unlikely that swinging the shovel at them will achieve much and he's not going to talk his way out of this one. They move in.

Bishop's weed, goutweed, snow-on-the-mountain, herb Gerard, devil's guts, *Aegopodium*, goat's foot, ground-elder: it's all the same medieval pot-herb the Romans brought, used for healing gout, sciatica and as a sedative for arthritic and rheumatic pains. Slightly laxative and diuretic, young leaves in salads, cooks like spinach. It is the perfect garden weed: beautiful, tough, irrepressible and invasive. Never gives up. Ground-elder rhizomes creep around the edges, find the cracks and infiltrate the roots of dormant plants.

He can't shake off this feeling of threat. However hard he tries to get rid of it, there's a fragment of that dream inside him, a growing fear of being overtaken by a terrible, impending danger.

Hogweed

In fields of the western moon, where Mill Lane crosses the tin bridge below the junction of the line to Wolverhampton and the old track to Donnington depot: my great-grandfather worked the signalbox here which is now a dry patch of ballast and birch trees. Above the junction are two abandoned fields surrounded by new roads, school grounds, housing estates, scrapyards and car showrooms. The view north drifts into the Weald Moors and south, beyond the church tower, is the Wrekin and its wooded hills.

These are the fields open to loss, where peewit and partridge have fled. Fireweed, thistle, ragwort, centaury, meadowsweet and a violet ground beetle; angeldust of grass pollen, crickets and the mad tunes of bees and crow ghosts wrung from dark poplars. They are here, displayed before the young arsonist in a dream, dog-placed, washed up on a tide which gathered back in time and crashed here to be sucked down to the dark reaches of the earth.

It's a warm bright start to the day. To the people going to work in cars and trains, this looks like a scruffy green bounded by road and railway which, more by luck than judgement, avoided being built on. But to the early-morning wanderer, soaked with dew, this is a place of wonders.

Fields liberated by neglect, freed from agricultural oppression, a flowering waste: brilliant carmines of fireweed, brass of ragwort, purple of thistles. A goldfinch chants from overhead powerlines, throwing his evocation across the flowers for the promise of seeds to feed his tribe later. Hogweeds that caught the rain, pumped themselves high into great cumulus umbels of pink and white, providing erotic stages for mating soldier beetles, now fold the year into a tiny bus ticket tucked inside each offered pip.

The sun inches higher and the daytime life of the flowering rough begins to bustle. The scrapyard across the tracks clangs into life, iron cockcrow from another world.

Black knapweed

Knapweeds in October: along the coastal footpath above tankers slipping in and out of Pembroke, a brownstone sea cliff, half-baked like bread, half-drowned like kelp. Old flowers in a brown nap, once purple but called 'black', they bottle summer rain from the Celtic Deep in flasks of seed waiting to be spilled into the grass of St Anne's Head.

Across the Dale Roads at night, the lights of a funfair with no fun: Milford Haven refineries glitter with the glamour of stars but by day look like a forest of dead trees in sea mist.

Down in Dale, Musselwick Bay butts against the wall in front of The Griffin and ball floats mark the crab pots. How bright – DayGlo yellow, pink, orange, like florists' blooms chucked in the sea. But there are dark buoys knocked round like heads knapped awkwardly turning this way and that, tethered to some appalling wreck the crabs are picking at way below.

French bean

He parked by the river and walked through old narrow streets at dusk to the shop by the village green. Inside, baskets of vegetables surrounded a large central table and women waited to be served. He picked up fistfuls of French beans and put them into brown paper bags. In his hands they began to feel like meat and he had to open the bags repeatedly to check they really were beans. In the half-light of the grocer's, the beans lay in their paper bags like sticks or bones waiting to be cast. In Green Cloud temple on Julan Tokong Street in Melaka where he shook *kau chim* oracles, fortune sticks rattling in a bamboo cylinder, one stick emerged from all the others with a corresponding slip of paper on which was written a worryingly ambiguous portent. The French beans were similarly ominous. Meanwhile, the woman serving at the central table was taking ages. She carried a customer's bags out to a big yellow tractor and drove off in it to deliver them. When she returned she continued to ignore him and served the other women in the shop instead. Exasperated, he said he would wait no longer, dropped the beans on the table and walked out not knowing whether the sigh he heard on closing the door was one of admiration or relief. When he got back to where he thought he parked his car, there was an old Morris thousand with its bonnet up. He peered into the darkness where its engine should have been. Men were approaching across the car park. Merde! He had only seconds to reach his own car and drive the hell out of there.

Rosebay willowherb

On the A4169, just over the brow of the hill where the verge widens before the gateway down to Shadwell Quarry, it shows its true colours. Blown by the swiping wake of lorries piled with larch-lap fencing, the down has drifted off like steam rising from the tilth of fields across the road. Now liberated from growing and flowering and seeding, it is free to show the glorious trauma which earned its title, 'fireweed'. Scarlet, crimson, sienna, umber, tangerine: its blitz colours burn along the roadside above a gutter-mulch of ash leaves and stubborn grass. Rosebay follows traffic and fire. It sets up camp in the damaged places and, like a new memory which hides an old loss, bits of fluff make willowy stems and the carmine flowers of August. Now it stands in autumn, still and stiff for a bonfire moment before its leaves drop and brittle sticks snap from roots which suck the toxic sweat of roads on their journey from the bombsites.

Black bryony

Merridale Street after midnight, behind Mr
Singh's shop, sleeping in his van on yam crates;
Limpy pissing against the front wheel veering
homeward; the woody earth-torpedo yams that
smell of the Caribbean, paused on their way
to Wolverhampton market. Along the autumn
English lanes, old twists of string with swags of
amber berries in the hedge are black bryony;
they're yams too.

Bryony stems twitch like asparagus spears
in spring from the green hedge and grow all
summer into sprawling vines to dry like sisal
after flowering and only the berries remain. From
white, through orange to crimson, berries brighten
with promise but are full of poison. Underground,
the tubers are fist-sized, black on the outside,
yellow inside: powerful, acrid and cathartic
medicine which cures a bruise, a black eye.
Bryony root's older story is all but forgotten.

Black bryony is a 'womandrake', the female
equivalent of mandrake whose narcotic

hallucinogen trips back through centuries to the shrieking root dug from under gallows. The root of mandragora takes human form, a manikin, a puppet for the earth magic of old Europe. Because mandrake doesn't grow along English lanes, people here looked for alternative demonic manikins to dig up and found the bryonies. White bryony, the only British member of the gourd or cucumber family, became a substitute mandrake. Black bryony, the only British yam, became womandrake. Both plants are poisonous.

Exhume the root-woman: would you recognise her wandering the lanes, waiting at the bus stop, queuing in the supermarket? See her through her reflection in the television – yam-head! Self-medicated, the absence in her gaze is because her mind travels the dark spaces under streets, under hedges, in the underworld. The womandrake of hedge religion bursts from the thicket at night and flies above the lanes, laughing. She sweeps owl-like across roofs, round the tower of St Peter's church and over the market hall, delirious. Limpy looks up on Halloween Night and makes a wish.

Devils-bit scabious

Sitting in the porch – between an iron-studded
oak door and the arch which framed a view
across flagstones to a low wall, down a lawn to
the old yew tree, over fields to alders bordering
the brook then onwards along Hope Edge – he
wanted to feel the same as he did sitting there
when he was ten. All those years ago, lacing his
boots with other walkers and socialist cyclists,
it was a moment he would always remember.
And yet there was nothing to it. Socks, dubbin,
oilskins, corduroy, camaraderie, ways through
open land leading to old hostels like this with no
electricity or running water but ghosts, bunks,
folded blankets and the smell of ox-tail soup.
His daughter was coming through the new door
which kept the central heating in behind the
old studded one. She had a daughter the same
age he was when, sitting next to his father, he
laced the memory of this place on his feet. Many
generations sat on the porch shelf, putting their
boots on, ready to walk out in hill weathers.

Smoke up the chimney, rain down the brook, the dust of journeys pressed in these old stones. No, he couldn't feel the same. He'd had that moment: a flower as blue as a liquorice allsort in summer meadows long ago. Now he was returning through cold, wet earth. It was winter, the dream that rooted him there bitten off.

Basil

They slept listening to the breathing, afraid the
breathing would stop. *Lucerti! Lucerti!*[*] Ruin
lizards ran on the steps of a little cave house called
The Tomb where she was born. Snow covered
the Etai Mountains like milk. At night it was too
dark for birds to sing. The only light came through
a gap under the door and lit a few dried leaves
of basil.[†] Even far away, she would forever live
within the magnetic fields of that place. This was
the omen on the first full moon in March.

[*] Lizard in Sicilian dialect.

[†] 'The basil tuft that waves / Its fragrant blossom over graves.'
From 'Light of the Harem', *Lalla Rookh*, Thomas Moore
(1779–1852)

Little Toller Books

We publish old and new writing attuned to nature and the landscape, working with a wide range of the very best writers and artists. We pride ourselves on publishing affordable books of the highest quality. If you have enjoyed this book, you will also like exploring our other titles.

Field Notes

Monographs

Nature Classics Library

A postcard sent to Little Toller will ensure you are put on our mailing list and amongst the first to discover our latest publications. You can also subscribe online at **littletoller.co.uk** where we publish new writing, short films and much more.

LITTLE TOLLER BOOKS
Lower Dairy, Toller Fratrum, Dorset DT2 0EL
W. littletoller.co.uk **E.** books@littletoller.co.uk